≡ NIGHT TRAIN ≡

NIGHT TRAIN
POEMS BY
W. LORAN SMITH

PLINTH BOOKS
WEST HARTFORD, CONNECTICUT

Manufactured in the United States of America.
Printed on acid-free paper.

Direct inquiries to the publisher:

PLINTH BOOKS
P. O. Box 271118
West Hartford, CT 06127-1118

FIRST EDITION

Library of Congress Card Catalog Number: 96-69876

ISBN 1-887628-00-2 (cloth)
1-887628-01-0 (pbk.)

Cover and interior design by Charles Casey Martin

For my wife Susi, and my children Ben, Rachel, and Loran, whose light keeps me going through the catacombs.

≡ ACKNOWLEDGMENTS ≡

Grateful acknowledgment is made to the editors of the
following publications and presses where many of these
poems first appeared:

CHAPBOOKS
Avernus (White Fields Press)
The Boy Who Became a Book (*Thinker Review*
Chapbook Series)

PERIODICALS, ANTHOLOGIES, RECORDINGS
Kansas Quarterly
"A Day If That"
"Butchertown"
Last Call (anthology, Sarabande Books)
"Sole of Dover"
"The Family Man"
"Butchertown"
The Louisville Review:
"Carmina"
"Soul in Three Parts"
Omphalos (spoken word CD, Rant/Literary Renaissance)
"Big Sur"
Thinker Review
"Vessels"
"Clapboard Towns"
"In the Coming of Gravity"

Also, my gratitude to Jim Finnegan, my dear friend, who has faith in these words.

≡ CONTENTS ≡

THE FAMILY MAN

There are men so crazy from not having something,
that they build temples to it, and walk under the groins
and spires, chanting to the emptiness of it, and when night
unrolls its mattress for their pallet, they put a picture
of it on the table, and lie down pretending it has come
to keep them warm in its green sparkling dress,
with the mink head on the shoulder, curling back its viscous lip.

There are men so crazy from not having something,
that they dress their daughters in blue skirts and white tights,
and take them to the circus where the children squeal
at the clowns bumping and tumbling in their eyes.
So crazy, they promise their daughters white-plumed horses,
and cotton candy, and pinwheels of happiness forever.
And then these crazy men go home, and while the house
is four ticks of their antique clocks, and two winter breaths,
they close the garage door, lie down on the front seats
of their Chevys and let the engine sing its sweet song.

There are men so crazy from not having something,
they drive to a bar in Albuquerque, and laugh
at the lewd cartoon napkins of big-chested women
leaning over just so. They sit there for years
until she sidles up and, claiming to have it, bends
her legs back, and lets him taste the juicy red eye of it.
There are men so crazy that George Jones is their hero,
and while, *"He stopped loving her today,"* plays on the radio,
they wash down the pills from the silver turquoise locket,
and see God's blue face, blank and pure above the buttes.

There are men so crazy from not having something,
they marry prom queens at the Love Forever Chapel,
and then for twenty years slap their silly faces for looking
at them while they eat, and the kids listen through
the ears of the honey-yellow walls to their father's voice
making their mother a tiny, dried-up flower, all light
and shed of skin when she comes to kiss them in the dark.

There are men so crazy from not having something,
that they become women and stick their fingers into
the wet, dark cave of themselves to feel the ribs
of where they were pulled out by the stainless steel tongs,
and wrapped in cotton receiving blankets, and taught
by the nurse to take the rubber nipple without choking.
So crazy like this, that they smell the kinky black hair
under a woman's arms, and become insane with a memory
like a hand thrusting up and up again through the icy water.

There are men so crazy from not having something,
that in one day, nothing and everything is it.
The wafer of moon burning in their foreheads is it,
and the Uncle Sam in his red and white rags waving
a novelty flag at all the cars on Fourth Street,
and wives who give it away they have so much of it,
even the slobbering smiles of their black dogs are it.

There are men so crazy from not having something,
that their bones are it, and the muscles of their hearts
are it. The eyes, the night, all of the night and the path.
The light and Christ are it. The cells flying off their fat
bodies are it. The gallery of suits, the needle's last rites,
the governor playing golf and the phone not ringing are it.
The crow engulfing its own huge shadow,

the grass, the insects, the wars, the missile biting
into the children's ward. Everything is crazy with it.
Wanting it, dreaming it, sucking it, needing it,
until all the tunnels and the ends of the earth are it.

A GOOD MAN'S FATE

At a quarter-of-five in the morning a sparrow worries
the mulch underneath the porch light, as my father
lights a cigarette and stands by the Dutch door in the kitchen
watching the pale eye of moon fade away.
In his half-eaten brain, the first flame of vodka moves
with only potential through the ruins of his simple wishes,
and he is sure God's voice is a thousand birds singing
between this dark and light. He is sure that his wife
will call him to her bed, where he will finally press himself
against her back, his perfect cock nestled between her legs.
Her nipples hard from the spit he has licked onto his fingers.

At a quarter-of-five in the morning my father
is the saint of emptiness, he washes clean all the world's
trouble in that first swig. There is so much to believe in,
that his gut burns with the pain of not loving it enough.
And he knows full well how hearses purr and wind their way
down the manicured hills, and how many tons of dirt
it takes to cover the whirling polished atoms of a cherry casket.

My father is a visionary, he can see his pores bleed
their grayness before our very eyes. How soon, his grandson
will wait all day for him to rise and take him down by the river
to watch the tugboats go churning by. You were great, Father,
how you divined those waters of the dead, the way you held
the quivering willow branch over your soiled sheets,
over the mumbling of our names, over the thick
muscled arms of the nun who prayed by your bed.
The way you fulfilled all your prophesies like a king.

SOLE OF DOVER

On my parents' honeymoon, my mother stood not
ten feet away from the one and only Frank Sinatra,
who was swaying at the blackjack table, dead drunk
and pissed at being ten thousand down, pissed
at this little shit who's been betting against him
all night, making snide comments behind his back.
So when he says something really sick about Frank's wife,
he turns and lays the guy out on the plush casino carpet.
Blood everywhere and all the people slapping Frank
on the back. All this happening, when my mother
has one of those epiphanies that hit you right
in the stomach, and she knows she will never love
my father who's back in the room sleeping off three
whiskey sours and a porter house steak. She thinks,
I shine and that will be enough, some fly boy will come
and take me, part my fine white flesh, flake me off
in tender forkfuls. Thought she was the sole of Dover,
my mother did, as Frank brushed by her, letting his
hand rest for just a second on her hip.

Two days later when they're driving through the desert,
they hear on the radio about this small-time hood
who's found in the trunk of a late model Ford,
parked out back of the Sands Hotel. My father tries
to describe how they always make a rookie pry it open,
this comic rite of passage when his head snaps back.
But my mother feels like puking, never really puts two
and two together. She thinks Frank shines and that will
be enough, that he will come and take her to that small

town park. And all the little boys will stop and look
while the football floats through the twilight sky.
Then later the moon will stream down through the slats
of a gazebo, burning into his tan muscular shoulders.
She thought, I shine and that will be enough.
How the satin makes them quiver and the stars come
out at night. Thought she was the sole of Dover, my mother did.

THE TROWEL LEFT IN A PASTORAL SCENE

My grandmother was not asleep in the blood-red leaves,
having been picked up outside of Shiply's diner
where she waited tables, waited for Hank Williams
all dressed in white to come unsteadily in the door.
He might have looked like Hank, yodeling
to the radio as they drove, drove along the river road.
And from what I've heard, the sheriff guessed
she had it coming, the penis that is, not the knife
that slit her like a jukebox kicked with a lizard boot
and a thousand songs tumbling out. The river of coffee
she had poured while thinking, "Those boys at their
daily table, their daily hot roast beef sandwiches,
kinda look sick and dying in the polished chrome reflection
of this pie case." As they leaned in, motioning
to my grandmother, whispering a tad too loud,
"I'd sure like to fuck me one of those Indian gals!"
Maybe she could have pulled herself up and rode
her way to their fat pumping hearts. Maybe she was trying
when that cowboy slid in real fast. Maybe she had
some sudden faith in Mankind, the way the roll of twenties
bulged in his pocket, maybe it looked like rent,
or T-bone steaks, fat crackling on the grill,
a real birthday cake with fourteen candles for her daughter.

My mother, Anna Lee, waited by the window a long time
for some miracle to come sailing down.
But the neon sign flashing, *POOL, POOL, POOL,* and
the plain one that said, *World's Greatest Chili!,* must have
obstructed the view, a blur in God's peripheral vision.

They didn't find my grandmother for almost a year.
Probably didn't look real hard either, with her reputation
and all. Rumor had it she'd split with some gambler,
and was betting on the ponies in the Hialeah sun.
But one frosty night, a dappled German short-haired pointer
padded in from the woods, head down and bobtail twitching,
and made his way past the parlor and upstairs
to a farm boy's room, where he lay at the foot of the bed
and gnawed a yellow femur bone. And that farm boy
tried to listen to the Scriptures being read downstairs
by the fire, he tried to listen above the infernal slobbering
of his dog. He felt a breeze coming in the crack of the window,
and felt God out there in the dark, like a beacon,
like a light, like the cows in the Jesus barn.
PASTORAL, was the word they had learned
in school today, as in peaceful and spiritual,
as in flocks and herds, and shepherds who watch
over these. Not the same gods whom the cows
spoke of in low and tender voices to their kneeling calves,
sweet breads bulging in their necks, not the gods
who wore blood-spattered T-shirts and *"Sawed*
you in half, . . . yes, in half, my love, and the trick never,
ever, works." But what faith do cows have,
and my mother ran along the Portland Canal
hooping and hollering, while the wild boys ate her up.
Their flesh at fifteen mistaken for a mother's kisses
in her belly. Because, you see, she wanted
something you can grow, something of her own,
something more tender than a maggot growing
on the donations from the Women's Club.
Something you can see, unlike the angels driven
through the heads of flowers, something you can leave

18

and see if anyone in the world will weep. A doll like me
inside her stomach, a warm and floating poem,
An open window / White and purple lilacs / The baby cries.

THE LAST HOUR OF THE MONARCH

I try to remember it all correctly,
as my wife and I drive to the Abbey of Gethsemane,
over these worn-down hills engulfed by thirty years
of kudzu, like some demented Magic Kingdom,
the bright oriental leaves bending
and flowing over the crests of abandoned barns.

I try to remember how the handsome,
young novitiate glanced up into the abstract light
pouring in through the windows of the cathedral
to see my wild wife's bare breast in the balcony,
purple and ripe as cheese melting in his mouth.
But she is born-again in Texas now,
taking computer classes, asking forgiveness in malls,
her past whispered at night in God's huge ear.
But he was by her side all the time.
I saw him the night she tied off our arms
in the bathroom, and let the teaspoon of nectar
slide into the pain we beat down,
the warm tiles sliding under our feet,
under our bodies where we lived to fuck,
until our lives were nothing more.
Here too, at this holy spot, we fucked,
Holsteins munching slowly toward our moan,
angels droning in their monarch skins,
against the slap and sweat of brainless light.
But I am driving over the lull of Kentucky's
hills with another woman now, this good earth

of a woman beside me, who holds me down
so gently by the thinnest strand of silk.

We drive in our silent gardens of desire
knowing that we are strange vessels now,
carrying our two children over the sea.
We pass the garden in the woods,
where another child lies, a thumb of a daughter,
rowing all night while I held her mother.
Past our own fathers, those garage men,
and whiskey drinkers, alone with the steel
of their hammers and wrenches,
cursing the ratchets of their bruised, cut knuckles.

These Trappists sway among the white pines,
drop like seeds settling into crevices.
And where my child is buried, Mary holds
her own boy, a splattering of blood
on her *chador*, eyes like roses
in the metal light of her body.
I have planted a garden too late again
this spring, but in my dyslexic brain,
I give thanks for the stalks and leaves,
and the buds' tight little fists of color.
Time moves so slowly with nothing
but peace to conquer.

TO SEE IN THE FOURTH DIMENSION
THAT HE WAS AS BEAUTIFUL AS EVE

—Kurt Vonnegut

Joseph wakes, when everything seems to hold a purple, breathless piece of sky, and dawn rushes over the sea, over the Dover cliffs the sweep and curl of gulls set on fire. Sun is on the thatched roof, on the Calvary cross-beam passion of barns in its light. The milk maids' thighs are open for creamy buckets of cow gushing down, and the sleepy children smell of pansies and honey. It is morning. Below him in the courtyard, Joseph hears the men pounding at the forge, the spark of worlds grunting, spitting serpents into the ground. Joseph rises to tend the hearth, to fan the faggots into flame. The grindstones whine now, knives pressed against their spin. It is almost Christmas. Joseph shivers on the cobbled hearth, legs pressed together, the line of buttocks tight beneath the muslin robe. It is morning. In the stable, farm boys wake, hands on weasels hard as oak under the patched cloth. Rag-headed women count their bags of herbs, rose-nippled mushrooms smelling like the moon.

I am Joseph, Royal Cook's Assistant. The farm boys catch them in silky nets at dusk. There are thousands of them waiting in those leather bags. I snip the long black tongues of larks, of sparrows, partridges, pigeons, blue-green whispers of hummingbirds, necks all broken with a sly-boy crack. I am Joseph. At night, I dream of banquets stretching through the velvet wood. Mile after mile of blazing candelabra, black tongues placed like jewels in a sea of crimson aspic. Eyeballs make the stock, hooves to powder make it stick, this is my life. I am Joseph, Royal Cook's Assistant. I snip red throats still filled with songs, and behind me in the bed, that is Margaret, Irish Margaret, rosy-cheeked Margaret, skin like butter Margaret, hallowed Margaret rolling into my warm spot for a moment more of sleep. It is almost Christmas time. I am Joseph, Royal Cook's Assistant, revered among the silver-backed sage, the golden yarrow, the blessed thistle. I take the songs of birds and grind their hollow bones. That is Margaret behind me. She rubs my rooster and I cock and crow, I kiss her Blarney stone, morning comes, and everything holds a breathless piece of purple sky. The child beside her smells of pansies and honey. I am Joseph. I tend the hearth and go to work. I snip the songs of broken birds.

NAMING US

"You know, they never married," my aunt told me
as we stood staring at my mother's gravestone,
the closest I had been to her in thirty-seven years.
And across the bottom it reads, *"Wife,"* put there
by the man who begged her to marry,
took care of her like a baby until the end.

Who's to argue in a graveyard about what waiting
will do, but I think the least you could have done
was to be buried miles back in the hills.
Down a dark road with giant willows closing
the light off overhead, then suddenly there it would be,
your grave nestled in the shadow of a small stone church,
and so many wild roses and moss growing over your name,
that I would come and trim them each week.
Pull them from the earth, my hands bleeding,
the thorns tearing into the pink translucent cells
that held something so close to memory all this time.

Something as far away as the seed that formed
in your teenage belly, the weight that came slowly
into those savage cheekbones.
Both of us could call this faith, I guess.
Whatever it is that wakes us, says go on.
To rise the morning they came and took me,
your father yelling, and you holding me like a child
might hold a toy, saying, *"Mine, Mine."*
You could call this faith, I guess.
That first night away from you,

24

the watchman's white beam streaming down
on the rows of cots in the county children's home.
Each face turning from the light, each bed sailing
into its own perfect definition of alone.

But I will come, Mother. Like the old ones you see
in the cemetery, windbreakers much too thin
for the weather, bent and talking to the part of them
that's buried. I will come to this plain patch of field
by the huge sign of *Sam's Carpet Barn*,
by the metal whining of the expressway
that has tried to take me to you a thousand times.

SOUL IN THREE PARTS

It is Halloween today.
In a driving rain I go to you, the leaves
washed down like ruby-gold Spanish galleons.
These pockets of little demons rush
across the street, swept to the door,
with vanilla and immortality on their breath.
A perfect hoedown for death's fiddle.

It would seem you like it here.
The slate-colored juncos, the ego of black swans
paddling viciously around the fountain.
When no one is watching, I ask where you
have hidden the jewels, tell you another woman
will be my queen of seaweed, my queen of death.
But I know you have nothing to offer,
memory all decayed, bunched up in a dense husk
of roots. There is so little to hold as a chalice.
I can say, you liked the woods, could fix
almost anything, and once I saw you cry, when
you clubbed the nest of rabbits caught in the mower.
But then the years and years of carrying you
from the car, the sound of bottles clanging,
in all your secret hiding places.

The things you've missed.
How easy for children to hate the dead.
But now, I am blessed again, his head dropping
low into her cervix. We lie down together,
oblivious as the world passes over us.

Our hearts are as pure as the Amish children
in that picture that hangs above your desk.
They are walking home from school
in a cradle of light that defies the low black
clouds behind them, stalks of corn waving
on either side of the dirt road. I call out to one
of the children, who turns from the others,
and laughing, runs towards me.
This is the only vision I can offer.
You know those man-thoughts, Father,
those defined spaces cut off from air,
when we are left so little of our beginnings.

TENDERNESS

If I saw that water-headed boy today,
who used to stumble down the hall at school,
his hands in front of him to ward off our blows,
I think I would tell him, *"It is furious and tender
here in God's neighborhood."* Yes, that is what
I would say. But it's way too late for that.
The cardinals sit like drops of blood in the apple tree,
and we sweet-faced children who hailed you
in the hall, we are diamonds in our own right,
cut to suffer, too. We lie down to sleep,
with brimstone under our nails, and pray to God,
pray to Blake, that some angelic form our wanting takes.

Because who could have imagined that when we kicked
the neighbor's dog, or when I threw that rock
and broke the seagull's back and watched it fall.
Who would have known how we would still feel
the edge of stone separate the skin, the howling
and yelping in the corner of the garage.
But we little boys, we have lizards in our brains,
we always want to sway on the back porch,
with a warm bottle of sweet strawberry wine,
the iron rails rusting in the heat, and the silhouettes
of the Marys and Leslies undressing in their rooms.

So now my friend the bookseller, and my friend the poet,
we gather to drink coffee, try our best to ignore
the androgynous girls, their pelvises itching like
blackberries along the stone fences in County Wicklow,

spikes and nose rings bursting in the dark.
But our wisdom never gets as hard as that,
our brilliant conversation goes nowhere fast.
The lizard always seems to get its way, crossing the road,
past God's yard with its score of lightning bolts,
blinking faintly against his house, and when you turn
to look at me on this cold rainy morning,
I am still standing nonchalantly against my locker,
waiting for you, knowing you will flinch and wobble.
So furious and tender through it all.

BIG SUR

We're stroking now,
     I mean this day is unbelievable,
Big Sur, Big Scene, Big Curve,
     Big Sun dropping in a delicious sky.
Right off this cliff where we stop,
     My lady's singing Neil Young to a caravan
of Dead Heads heading south for some "Business,"
     and I'm thinking maybe we could move
right next door to some rock star who's made
     his money on digital and tits,
Manhattan gold.
     I'm thinking about some poets I know,
thinking how they're not groovin',
     lives being chaos and such,
initials in a big confession soup.
     I'm thinking about some poets I know,
obese heads like a butcher's loose,
     set free to chopping there,
blind men in the forest of Kafka's trees
     see them fall, there they go!
STABILITY.... BEAUTY.... MEANING.

And sure, I'll admit to anything.
     Quiet desolation, lovers like rain,
sweet little girls and wet wicker dreams.
     I've strapped the needle to the heart's
embrace, heard that narcotic bell of love,
     And old Jimmy Beam done chewed me up,
but it's got to be some phenomenon,

maybe 'cause I'm white, went colonizing it,
driving on the wrong side of the road,
    just me and death, jet-black hair
flying in the wind like somebody cared,
    but nobody cares, just the wannabes,
people not groovin', brittle lives,
    adding to the confusion, and I'm thinking
about some poets I know, don't even see
    eyes turning in the park, you can't
even see them saying, "Fuck you," under their breath,
    'cause you're late for that Friday appointment
where you get to hate your mother.
    And that hungry little girl,
she ain't buying no poetry books,
    'cause they're lacking in some essential vitamin.
But what the hell, it provides a decent living,
    this air-conditioned nightmare,
this train pulling out of the station,
    full of poets, look at them juggle,
one .... two .... three .... four schools of thought
    just like that, like a one-hand clap,
don't mean nothing, don't say nothing
    to my lady singing here above Big Sur,
belly swollen like a sea of love.

HAIRSPRAY

It had to be about the hottest day of this bad year,
when Shanda Lee killed her little babies.
You could see it all at six o'clock, the cutter steaming
out in slow motion, the grappling hooks splashing
in the muddy water, and Shanda, she's sitting on the bank,
telling the reporters about her so-called life.
Said she wiped their asses to stop the screaming,
wrapped the stink and ooze in a plastic bag,
just like Momma had always taught her.

And though she's wet, her big fast-food belly clinging
to her shirt, and though she keeps pressing
this plastic, purple-maned pony to her breast,
like it's every girl's best and loving friend,
what we really want to see is some regret,
why she made them hold each other's hands,
pictures from her wallet, a hazel twinkle in their eyes,
some clover hair blowing in the wind. But we don't.
We just see this worn-out girl, a yellow shadow underneath
her eyes where Jimmy came to visit last Sunday,
and got so drunk, he thought her cow-eyed face
was the world he couldn't even begin to beat,
thought her throat was another dead-end job.

They hook one baby now, and next week the jokes
will fly around the fax machine, "What's red and blue,
and pops like a big balloon?" And then by the next week
we'll forget the whole thing, a mental inquest and the usual delays.
"Not that bitch again, they play it for all it's worth,"

until some other Shanda Lee, or Amber Sue,
holes up in a cheap hotel, and while the kids eat Cheerios
off the floor, she'll call every street punk she knows.
Like they're gonna give her a piece of the rock,
like blow jobs are hard to come by in this day and time.

And all those dreamy little babies with their tight curls,
they never learn you can't cry for wanting here.
So suck on your thumb, or beat your sister,
twist the arms off that robot hero, because nobody's watching.
Blame it on the hairspray, and for God's sake learn how
to unlatch the seat restraint. It's press in and pull out.
In and out. I hope you get it, 'cause it's getting old, these
dreamy little bloated children, and their petty woes.
And Shanda Lee is rocking ever so slightly now.
They found them both, and the sun is going down,
and the waves are lapping gently over the dog food cans.

IN THE COMING OF GRAVITY

All night long I have this dream that violets
are escaping from my eyes and mouth,
shattering against the window of my room.
In the morning I take one of my grandfather's
old books and walk to the end of our road
where the farm spreads out, the silver flash
of creek moving through its green belly.
I move past the goldenrod and the Queen Anne's lace,
past the thickets where we burrowed last summer,
whispering under the damp smoke of our cigarettes.

I cross the creek, past a slithering in the corner
of my eye, past the willow carved like a dangerous
old sailor, and the metal carcasses of toys poking
up through the mud, foreign to me now as lightness.
I have been reading furiously lately, two or three books
a week. Anything to stop the star I imagine is burning out
inside of me, whatever it is that has brought logic
to the equation of hills and trees I've abandoned.

Here is the thicket, and I crouch low, lower to enter
its passage, my chest scrapes against the roots,
and the light is streaming in between the brambles,
spreading out over my rust-colored hands that open
my grandfather's book. This book that is more famous
than I will ever be. And five hundred elephants are caught
in the pass, sinking to their knees in the deep snow.
The Carthaginian soldiers are beating them, Lord, how they
are beating them to rise. But a thousand bells will not wake them.

Even Hannibal prays in his gaudy tent, the whole world
rushing in with such sadness that I feel like my skin
has been peeled back to the core of muscles and nerves.
The air hurts so much in this coming of gravity.
Like now, listening to them carry your boxes to the truck.

THE STORY

This is the story of a boy who became a book.
For if he had not become a book,
then this would be the story of an egg abandoned
in some upstairs apartment above a bar,
the wind coming in through the usual cracks
of the cheap siding. An egg laid in swaddling rags
in a wicker basket set in the corner by the ironing board.
Instead of an egg though, the boy became a book.
A book of oversized ducks that could talk, and giants
whose feet would slip and fall through the billowing clouds.
He became a book, and moved to a lovely ranch-style house
built from war bonds. He had a mother and father,
who were shining examples of what prosperity
and millions dead will do for the victors.

This certainly seemed his big chance to become a boy,
but he remained a book, and at night, the tin thump
of the furnace kicked on and the voices drifted in.
But as a book, he barely felt the cold, and no matter
how much Scotch they drank, or even when they brought
bouillon and toast for his fevers, even then, they could never
get him to act like a boy. He was a book, and suddenly,
the Black Knight would appear out of nowhere,
thundering down the path, the thighs of his stallion
glistening in the pools of moonlight, the crested helmet lowered,
the lance pulled in tight to his side. You know the rest.
All those bodies stacked behind the castle.

Over the years he remained a book.
For if he was not a book, then he would become
a shadow walking after dusk in his neighborhood,
the speckled birds the boys had shot, fluttering in the bushes.
He found that even shadows are not happy among people,
that too often they catch the world in the fine gray
weave of their sweaters, an infinite number of sorrows
that became so sticky with people asking him to return
their affections, it was almost impossible to remove them all.
And if he was not careful, he would become an egg again,
squeezed between their soft hands, the perfect yolk of his soul
almost breaking. So it was much better to remain a book.
And over time he came to rest on the shelves of all sorts
of people, and sometimes, at night, when the fire was built
and the cat dozed off, they would come and stand in front
of him, naked like people do when they are in love.
They would stand there for what seemed like forever,
wondering if it were true, that no one had ever finished it.

ATOMIC

After that, it was never the same.
Geigers rattling all day, like boxes
of crickets clicking against the metal.
Even spring was properly valiant,
but the blossoms never opened.

Oh my child, your shadow is looking
so lonely. But look what I have brought,
your favorite nori rolls and jasmine tea.
Yes, we will have a picnic today,
and I will sing you all the old songs.

THE BUMS

Are disappearing where I walk.
Shoes and underwear swept into the coiled
barbed wire around the missions.
There are more of them gone every day.
Parchment roses floating in the oily puddles.
Gone from the loading docks and dumpsters,
from the lanterns of rusty barrels
that used to burn along the river bank.

There is no trick to vanishing.
One day a pain tears the heart,
a fist slammed into it, and suddenly,
we lie in our dreams, lips curled back
like dogs that hear a snap of wood,
a shoe scuffed against a broken bottle.
We fall on stone hands into wanting,
into suffering flowing from our bruised eyes.

And the coins jingle a little.
The photograph of a child fades.
The lone eye of God shines down,
his stiff fingers trembling in the cold.
The bums are disappearing.
Their clothes blown against the sides
of all the mute buildings,
where I walk to the bus along Market Street.

FATHER'S DAY

Sundays were visitation days.
The parking lot filled with rusty Monte Carlos
and all the parents, and step-parents,
waddling in with bags of underwear and socks,
the occasional jam box for a birthday.
And in the midst of all the explaining
their way out the door again,
I sat next to Mark, a twelve-year-old
Caucasian boy, his thin white arms
popping out at the elbows,
where his dad had twisted them
until they snapped and still twisted them.
Twisted them above a scream the whole neighborhood
must have heard, and turned the TV up.

This is for all the "You do what I say,
you little shit" fathers. This is for the short end
of wishbones and orange carpets
and children sitting in the sun, waiting
for their lives to take hold, for someone
behind them to steady the fishing pole,
for marshmallows to curl into syrupy
black goo that runs down your cheek,
and for a shadow bigger than love
to lie in the Coleman light and name
all the stars and constellations.

For the whole six months I worked there,
his family never wrote, or called,

or came to visit on those Sundays
of pressed pants and the smallest hint
of joy that radiated from the cinder blocks.
And that Sunday, on Father's Day,
Mark and I sat there in the sun,
my lungs gone flat as rice paper
with nothing to say, when he showed
me the card he'd made, the hearts
and the magic-markered "I love you dad"
running over the edge. This is for you Mark,
for your tight chinos, and slicked-back hair
on the corner of Fourth and Park
a year after I had quit, and my apartment
overlooked this corner where a steady stream
of men, of husbands, of lawyers, of doctors,
of priests, and antique dealers cruised and licked
their lips over the thin sweet boys of summer.

BUTCHERTOWN

The fine brick houses are crumbling,
falling after a hundred years of widows
skimming tallow off the creek, and teams
of Morgans whipped up these roads.
He told me today on the bus,
about the four thousand a day they kill,
how he knocks the horns clean off
when they stumble down the chutes.
He takes a swig of beer and shows me,
his huge black arms heavy with the hollow
crash against the back of my metal seat.

And I am flung against the railing blocks away,
wondering what he can tell his wife,
how much she can understand, when he comes
home at night, drunk like this, hands still warm
from the friction of steel, the rip of saws.
Wondering, if he wakes in the middle of the night,
and sees a line reaching from her belly to breast.
We are so far over the edge here,
that I feel the brush of wings, taste the blood
of wounded angels borne on simple pallets
through the town. I am the rat's eye in the hay.
And in those seconds after he swings,
my eyes roll back, and I can only ring the bell,
walk down the aisle, this part of me gone.

THE DEATH

In the foothills of the Ural Mountains,
an old dog turns and snarls at a light
shining from the window of a house
that stands in the small town square.
And if we looked in that window,
we would see a tall gaunt priest,
hovering over his book of gold letters,
and in the corner of the room,
there would be a mother holding her son's
frail head as he coughs into a white metal basin.

And above the house, above the sleeping town,
a hawk is turning and turning in a pure circle of flight.
Its black eyes looking down on the red clay tiles of the roof.

It is three o'clock in the morning.
The good doctor has come and laid his leeches
on the boy's soft skin, their round black mouths
whispering Latin into the marrow of his bones.
He touches the woman lightly on the shoulder,
bending down as if to say something.
Then shaking his head, he takes his hat from the bedpost
and softly closes the door behind him.

And above the house, above the sleeping town,
a hawk is turning and turning in a pure circle of flight,
the hollow filament of its feathers turning gray,
then blue as cornflowers against the mountains.

43

Now the mother leaves the side of her boy's crib.
She lights a small black cone of incense,
kneels and takes the basin of yellowish-red water,
raising it to her lips and drinking from it.
Sobbing, she takes the limp child in her arms,
and holds him tight against her breast,
as if she could nurture him for this journey.

BABY RED

Four weeks after our son is born,
a dead baby is found in the parking lot
of a local mall. He is nicknamed Baby Red
by the news people. It is never determined
exactly what was the cause of death.
Some say he died from the impact
of being thrown from the car onto the asphalt.
Others say he suffocated in the black plastic bag
they found him in, the sub-zero temperature
of late December. The coroner finally says
that he was likely alive though all of this,
and that his head was crushed by a car,
by the steady stream of shoppers rushing
in to exchange their Christmas gifts.
This makes for much better news,
and the search is intensified for his mother.

I am tired of our blindness. Of the plastic wreaths
wired to the light posts above his blue-wrinkled head.
Of the newscaster who confuses his television faces
and smiles once during the telling of the story.
What is it, that his mother could have done this?
Those cavities of her brain rotted that once
would have held the pink coo, the holiness of his light
against her breast? But then, I remind myself
that even my own life is almost all desire,
a loneliness for an indefinable lullaby,
and that killing is what we are good at. That our
opposable thumbs and large brains make all this possible.

And below our brown city, the limestone plates shift,
close like vault doors over the Irish Catholics burned
in the Know-Nothing riots. The maids, that have buried
fathers with scars deep in their leathery shoulders,
wait for the bus. Even the trees cut down where they swung.
And after forty years, I have no knowledge of how
this works. I take my son, and press a hot-house daisy
to his face, hoping that he can inch through some crack
in time, that somewhere in the fresh, clean city of his life,
he will call forth some ritual, some god, some voice
in this wilderness that I have failed so miserably to hear.

A SHORT LETTER TO GOD

There's a favorite singer of mine who said
you had to have been drunk when you waved
your hand over this, and that might be true.
But I'm sure you're waking now, Lord.
It just seems to take stone so long to move,
and you had to dream your alcoholic dreams,
sweat out all those pints of believing, those cymbals
and yellow flowers by your bed. And now, I'm sure
your beauteous angels are oiling their mechanical wings,
cherubs have taken up the flaming swords,
clanking along the battlements of your shining city.

We have waited so long for your chiseled pores
to sweat out the fever, everywhere bushes are on fire,
stones dissolving in the bellies of the evil.
But you are rising now, Lord, aren't you?
Why even the trains seem to move backwards,
piss flowing up the wet tracks, through the slats,
and back into the skeletons of Jews. And all the locusts
drop away from the sun, soldiers withdraw their swollen
cocks from the peasant women in the square,
suddenly back in their own beds, children tugging
at their beards. It will be such a miracle, *hosanna*.

I can almost imagine the cast-iron deer on the lawns
of your faithful raising a shy head and bounding into the wood.
The elements of satellites and missiles seeping
below a mountain meadow, and the bluebirds,
and wildflowers singing out your name.

It will be so wonderful when you can see your son again,
he's been screaming in the back room for centuries.
You can lay a blanket of stars over his wounds and kiss him
on the forehead with your perfect red lips.
I know it takes stone so long to move,
but I swear it's like it's already happened,
the neighborhoods filled with an *oh honey, honey beat,*
curving from my parents' bedroom,
around the big maple and into the garden.
And in the inner city, they'll pump up the holy jam.
No longer meet in dark suits, around the greens and corn.
All the bullets, like a miracle, spinning from the heart
back into the silver barrels of their guns.
Oh my sweet Lord, it's gonna be so glorious.

VERMONT

I'm passing these two college girls on the Ohio Turnpike
between Cleveland and Ashtabula, wondering why twenty
years ago no one gave a damn about sixteen-year-old brides,
when suddenly, a storm of black butterflies hits the windshield,
thick, as if God had spit them at me, the way their wings tore,
the yellow-green guts splattering everywhere.

Always one to believe in the potential of metaphors,
I think I might have to do something to justify it all.
And damned if I'm not sitting here in Vermont a few days later,
listening to a lecture on poetry and metaphysics,
when without warning, I feel like staying here forever.
Yeah, give me a scent and a drink and I'll lie down,
and there we were in this field of outrageously large clover,
her daring me not to touch her sun-splashed face.

But you are only a butterfly, I thought, my belly melting
with desire, my two fledglings crying for my return,
the optic fiber cables singing with my wife's voice,
stretched white across these lovely Vermont mountains,
over the barrels of maple syrup, the hot sap boiled down
and down and down until it was me driving home again.

Where being the center of everything, I decide I must be a saint.
But saints don't regret their holiness like this,
saints don't return home to see how dingy the city looks,
how the loop of taped church bells behind our house,
rings dull the same at midnight and at noon.

And my son sneaks up behind me and pulls a razor blade
through the pocket of desire. He takes such pity on me.

They know how addled I am, they kiss my stupid mouth,
stroke my low forehead, and my wife quietly mends
the tatters in my clothes, scrubs the stains in my underwear.
And while the shadows settle on the Legos and trains,
she sits by the bed, looks for the part of me that is missing,
she tastes the dust on my skin, the slightly bitter peaches.
Admires her red hair, shining in the morning light behind the diner.

NIGHT TRAIN

You call me today from the Healing Hands Shelter
on Market Street, and say, *"Hey, Bill, remember that
clear model of the human body we used to build as kids,
all the organs visible through the skin? Well, lately
people stop and stare at me, cover their children's eyes,
and just stare, brother, it's bad, can you pick me up
or something? I need a friend."*

Brother, I am your friend, but it's been seven years
since we've been together in those kitchen-sherry days,
the pissing days with our dark-eyed women to lay on the hands,
and I've quit drinking, married me a woman who is like
the sun coming in a dusty window, and when I pass my hand
through that beam of light it bounces and separates,
and always comes back together to its source.
I don't talk about those days, 'cause I have a backyard
with two apple trees and walnuts to shell on winter nights
while the kids tumble by the fire. It's all so fragile, my friend,
'cause God put a great big hole in us and never told us
how to fill it up, and everything they give me, it falls and falls
and there is no bottom, and before they know it,
I make them hostages, and then go out into this infinite
flowering world where the rocks and trees speak to me,
and see my friend in his tiny wheelchair in the park,
who married his blind princess. She pushes him through
the leaves, and he makes up songs for her about every living,
glowing thing that she can imagine, and when I return home,
my girl raises her head, her blond fly-away hair askew,
and a drop of breast milk frozen on her sleepy cheek.

But both you and I still won't be humbled,
won't be anything except a hole where all electrons
gather with their terrible hunger for a soul.
Mine is in my belly to be exact. My mother put it there,
then left with a clicking of heels down the corridor,
and a promise to come back. And for millions of individual
seconds I have counted sitting on the corner with a scratchy,
stuffed animal I named Tiger, and let everything come to me,
whole universes have been born with pin-pricks of stars,
and still nothing, friend, there is nothing there at all I need.
But right after the white explosion of our coming, when
she can still hold me, I see how beautiful it would be.
And I don't want to be alone again, I want to learn how
you hold a hand, brush the hair, sit beside the bed,
singing hymns, and feel every curve and crease and line
of a life together, the forehead wet with kisses.
I guess I want this, my friend, to be unashamed and visible
in the end, the room hot with my family's gathering.

VESSELS

Even in the shadow of steel, my eyes want to close,
half-drunk under this overpass.
But there is still so far to go, Jacksonville, Tampa,
the long white stretches of Florida, gorgeous blonds
rising out of convertibles to snap pictures of the egrets.
There is no solace here, the lizards are sucked dry
on the roadside, little wrinkled purses of exhaust.
Even the barmaid last night, with her bucketful of sex,
speaking in tongues on the cheap carpet, means nothing.
And big man that you were, finding her gun under the bed,
putting the bitter metal in your mouth, kissing it,
half hoping it would blow you away, is not enough.
Even that your father is dying and all you could
hear was that elixir of morphine, the halo that burned
around it all night. And it's not enough to have friends
like the ex-Marine and his dwarf brother who picked you up.
And later on the boardwalk, the three of you tearing
into the bouncer at that yuppie bar, the dwarf's wizened hand
sticking a pen knife in the football player's head,
the shiny tendon pulsing in his arm. There is no solace.

Then you woke the next morning on the beach,
a gelatinous stink of sea urchins washing up in the surf.
Up by the snack bar, you notice the gulls circling
around a little fat boy who is throwing bait into the air.
But it isn't fish at all, it's the pull tabs from cans he's collected
from the garbage, and at the same time a drop of something
hits you on the arm, then another, and suddenly there
are ribbons of blood falling on the beach around you.

You look up to see this old gray gull struggling in the easy
currents of wind, its mouth bleeding from the sharp edge of metal.
There is nothing to hold you anymore, the center is gone.
You remember the cheap stuffed toy your son keeps by his bed,
the flashy wooden ponies on the merry-go-round,
his high-pitched laughing, how it went faster and faster,
until his eyes pleaded with you to stop it, locking into yours
with each turn, and how you almost rushed to shut off the lever.
But you didn't. And later he still forgave you,
fell asleep in your lap driving home, his bright cheek,
the long black lashes closing, the dark wings of your life
lifting for a moment, letting you into that small passage
of the infinite. And then it was gone.

AVERNUS

*A volcano in Italy purported to be the mythical
entrance to the underworld.*

So I hear you're in Russia now, girl.
We must be getting old,
you trading in Baudelaire for the Bible,
and me, I'm in the literary world.
Sipping tea and letting them fire that cannon
up my butt, Bishop, Lowell,
and little Miss Plath
with her head in the oven,
about as wild as it's gonna get.

Hear you're in Russia now,
preaching to Chekhov's cousins
on that one-way ticket to God.
You, whose own road was so littered
with dead roses, I needed skin-tight
leather pants to show me to the gate.
And the morning after I met you,
I woke up forgetting I even had a baby
or a wife, kids in the lot behind us,
grinning with their paint-thinner smiles,
and Mother Dread next door,
screaming Ritalin down her blond-haired child.
But hey, that's more than some of us got.
All our friends just kept flaking off,
like the cheap metal on a cooked spoon,
while we lay in your water bed,
counting the thousand dollars
your sugar daddy brought.

We kept his naked picture in some book
by Genet, until he pissed you off,
and you took all his letters back
to his school-teacher wife, marched right
into her classroom wearing that necklace
with the baby-bird skeletons and dumped
them all in her lap, the whole first grade
all wide-eyed and not realizing yet,
they had just seen the future Madonna of the streets.

I hear you're in Russia now,
those raw-boned boys wanting to lay
on the hands, open up your belly,
like your uncle did, one greasy finger
in your blue panties, saying, *"Shit, bitch,*
who's ever gonna believe a twelve-year-old whore."
They didn't, not in your neighborhood,
desires dribbling down their chins.
I hear you're in Russia now, preaching on the street,
lying on the dark side of the moon
with that pretty-boy Jesus, whispering in his ear,
"Avernus, Avernus," and him thinking it's gonna
be a breeze getting out of there.
Yeah, I'm real glad you finally found the way.

A DAY IF THAT

There are not many,
these few graces I try to hold,
turn as the light strikes them.
The bright attention of a wren today,
shadowed behind the vine of leaded glass.
How she would read Sappho by the candle,
orange-scented thigh thrown across me.
The huge absolute of a moon over the cedars
where I walked in the dead of winter.
And once the peacocks I saw
rustling on a tin roof.
My son, who lay watching
the white moths fly blind from the grass.

This dream of a woman now.
A blue day among the leaves,
as we drive over the old hills,
fields snug up against the fences.
The half-hearted barking of dogs
rising in their duty.
I hold you and the skin sings of flesh
we can't remember, what's mine, yours.
The green breath of these cows
rising in the pasture.
My hand in yours, a sharp smell of pine.
The sun-furrowed stream below us,
that ripples *God . . . . God,* against the bank.

CLAPBOARD TOWNS

For Susi

This has been a lifetime.
I was the jawboned poet
sleeping with dogs and the rumbling
of trucks, nowhere else to go.
And then I tucked the girls in bed,
spread their legs and waited for something
to click, but when they turned for me,
there was nothing but the stars raining down,
the cry of children on the street.

I waited, thinking it had some shape,
some smell other than lying next to you,
the blue flash twisting in my spine.
Today I rose to the dervish of a hummingbird
dipping into the white begonias on our porch.
And while you sleep, the swans of Galway Bay
gliding through the reeds of your waking,
a crystal my son gave me, twirled from its cord.
A barely visible drop of color streaming down
on the plump ruby of your breast.
Saying everything I live for now,
is ascending at the burning speed of light.

LAST DAYS

I am sure someone is trying to kill me, and I suspect my wife.
Because recently, several times after we've made love,
and right before I go to sleep, I have seen her carrying
something that looks suspiciously like my brain down the hall.
And to make matters worse, I am almost sure that last month
I was only sixteen, sitting in the woods behind the house,
listening to the birds and trees whisper to each other
how beautiful I was, almost glowing with intensity, they said.
But now, suddenly, I am forty with two children banging
on something like sheet metal in the kitchen, the doorbell
is ringing, and this dog I never even knew I had is barking
incessantly in a shrill voice at the garbage men.

But proving that my dear wife is killing me, now that would
be another matter, indeed. For if I had the courage to follow her
to the living room where she sits on the couch with my brain
nestled in her lap, if I were to say something to the effect of,
"What have you done to my brain?" I know, like I know women,
that she would look up smugly and say it was only a magazine
she was holding so lovingly. Where would I be then?
I mean, who would I be to argue? For this is the way women
see things, something in their nature, this ability to embrace
life without thinking, this simplicity that is utter insanity.

Yet there she is, with my brain clearly in her lap,
a pile of black letters strewn on the floor, where she picks
and cleans my brain until the gray folds and delicate canals
are visible again. Now, I can accept that women like to peel off
anything their nails can grasp, but when she starts crying,

letting her tears fall down on top of my poor brain,
that I will have to ask her to stop. *"Can't you see,"* I will say,
"how ill my brain looks, how it flinches in this salt and air?"
But once again, I'm sure she will only lie, say it is a contact,
or a bit of dust caught in her eye. And if I asked her again,
"But what about those sixteen-year-old red-headed girls,
those, right there, on the carpet, the ones holding bouquets of flowers,
and intricately-folded notes against the hint of their breasts?"
She would only say, those are cobwebs, my dear husband,
look how they are sucked right up into the fan, and those bright
children you imagine playing kick-ball on the arm of the couch,
those are only reflections off my new gold earrings,
for I have no illusions of how swift and strong you used to be.
And if I said, *"But who is that lame old man gathering feathers*
on the beach to stick into the rickety frame of his wings, while
the world flies by so damn quickly, what do you claim that is,
    woman?"
Oh that, she would say, that is only a robin who hit the window.
Look, it is already dead, the flies gathering on its moist eyes.

AT THE WALT WHITMAN REST STOP
ON THE NEW JERSEY TURNPIKE

This city's hummingbird heart beats a muscular pulse
of lights and sparkle, of Styrofoam blown down
the streets like apple blossoms in spring.
And under the bridge to dull Camden town,
old mother, half-shepherd bitch, leaps out snarling,
the dark behind her squirming pink and blind,
the dark behind her squealing for the teat.
"The problem with reincarnation,"
Walt thinks, stumbling down the embankment,
rolling in the concrete shards and broken glass
to lie in a pretty green pool of antifreeze and oil,
"is, I can't remember one minute to the next who I am."
But Walt, I saw you cleaning windshields at the intersection,
holding the oily rag above the frightened faces,
the clicking of locks, the red vessels in your nose,
exploding on the glass. Your electric body convulsing
while you slept under the wires and cables that criss-cross
every inch of sky. I saw you look up at an uneven vee
of geese that honked and flew by, and, "Oh," you said,
"if I could only know myself."

Old Walt, purveyor of yourself, seller of your song,
I saw you on that corner, don't deny it, hood drawn down,
a tiny cellular phone in your huge palm pressed close
to your ear, as the planes rose and fell overhead.
Every five seconds they shimmered and shook,
rivets straining at the skin, bellies full of perfumed chatterers,
and silent ones writing *"Industry"* over and over in their datebooks.

And you were saying, *"Hey, baby! It's me, Little Tiny, I got the rock."*
Dull crystal in your pocket, and that bass box booming
a club mix of "Papa was a Rolling Stone." And behind you
in the pawnshop windows, cheap Japanese guitars twirled
on pedestals, spools of gold, sold by the foot or yard,
reeling off a terrible yellow light. Diamonds in their chipped clusters
lie on velveteen beds like prostitutes trying for their lives
to look clean and expensive. From the window of the Union Hall
a teenage girl in a polyester wedding dress watched you,
icing on her cheeks and eyebrows, while her virile husband
slammed down his fifth drink, and watched hoops
with his childhood buddies over by the bar.

Then you're born again, bloody child on our king-size bed,
growing more beautiful with every day I die a little more.
It's been a month without rain, the grass is worn, brittle as hay.
You push your Matchbook cars in impatient erratic circles,
half lying in the fine black silt around our picnic table.
The tree above us is scraggly and stripped of any bark
a boy your age could reach. But almost asleep now in the dirt,
you look up, like you do at least once a day. You turn to us,
hands outstretched, astonished, innocent of everything.
You turn and say, *"What is this? What is this place?"*
It amuses us, we laugh wearily, and I say, "Eat your pizza, Son,
because we have a long, long, way before we get home."

SATURDAY NIGHT

The man with no identification was hit on Saturday night
by a jacked-up dream of red-neck boys,
who just couldn't believe that some fag would wear
a woman's bathing suit and walk like that down the middle
of Taylor Boulevard, Brazilian string half-way up his ass.

They laid him out on Monday morning, laid him out
on a chrome trough table with fluorescent lights
shining everywhere and all the medical students trying
not to stare at his massive cock until the professor
had gunned his Jaguar out of the parking lot.
They roared in fraternal privilege and cut it off.
Passed it from department to department, still huge
after days of pasty manicured hands sliding uneasily
up the shaft. They hid it in the drawers of secretaries
right before they came in for work, bits of sweet potatoes
on their dresses and a dollar short in their red purses.
These pretty boys and girls take off their white coats
and dream at night of cadavers come to life, and brothers
coming home for Thanksgiving with everyone seated
around the crackling turkey, of brothers dressed in drag,
pill box hats and matching pumps and bags.

These Hippocratic boys and girls swear a little oath,
and never think of lovers, who called out, *Mother, Mother,*
and bolted for the door. Sleep, our good Samaritans,
so sure none of you were ten-years-old in the doorway
of your mother's room, everyone is gone and the shadows
dance across her bureau. Everyone is gone and the tiny ballerina

twirls on pirouette in the open jewel box, in the mirrored sea
of gold and silver costume trinkets. These cheap memories
that rise like a flood when he is hit by some jacked-up dream
of red-neck boys who just can't believe anyone
would take their mother's panties from the drawer,
overcome by the pink breeze and the sachet of roses.
Who can't believe that there are little boys who could never return
to the playground of little generals who taught them
how to bayonet, *"Yes, Yes....You twist it back and forth like that!"*

CARMINA

On April 15, 1989, in the Sonoma Valley region of California,
Ramon Salcido, presumably in a cocaine-induced rage, slit the
throats of his three young daughters. All three were found the next
day in a nearby landfill. Only the youngest, Carmina, survived.

I am Carmina, the one who lived.
The one who lay among the cuttings,
beside my sisters as the flies
gathered on their dark skin.
What I remember most is the cold floor
of his truck, when he had come and taken us.
He was screaming, *"Jesus! Jesus!"*
Teresa moved once, I remember that,
the blood gurgling from her throat.
But I was young, do you understand?
I was afraid to move to her.
I wanted to sing something Mama used to sing,
to hold them, but I was afraid.

But all that is a dream now,
all that is left is his face above me,
this man I hardly knew.
Now I can never leave him.
Hand in hand each night,
we walk down the hall.
He tucks me in, his kiss
cold and metallic in its craving.
Do you understand?

THE BEGINNING OF THE WORLD

When we were thirteen years old,
on a sweltering summer's day,
we all stood in Joey's basement.
And while his mother moaned
upstairs for her dying husband,
Joey took a latex glove from
the bomb shelter first-aid kit,
slipped it on and masturbated
his little dog Blackey.

Her son, oh her beautiful son,
he worked his two fingers
up and down, up and down.
Poor Blackey hunching under his hand,
eyes glazed, nails clicking
on the concrete, his little dart of a tongue
panting like a heart, while we howled.

And when his father died,
I was probably home whacking off
to a *National Geographic.*
The bare-breasted village women
showing me the golden nerve.

Or I could have just as easily
been in the woods,
convincing Leslie Gordon
to take off her cotton panties,
for a dollar and a pack of Necco wafers.

But I was only thirteen,
and the truth of the matter is,
it all smelled like lightning,
like the beginning of the world.

SOBER

Once the little birds of summer sang shyly, sweetly,
in the cedars, from which dripped amber sap
like fire on the cottage roof where I slipped the socks
off my wife's best friend. And my poor wife?
She was only seventeen then, empty and as pliable
as my dog's rubber chew toy. Tucked in real tight,
a clever trip wire of bottles around the couch
where she'd passed out. She might as well have been bound.
She's gone now, of course, and I'm sober now.
The great landscape of freedom opens up before me,
and my new family is sure that my tumbling brain
will settle down when I walk across their lives.
I love how everything we aren't becomes a metaphor for us,
how gently we speak of meaning in the amethyst eyes
of the mice and rabbits and deer on our walks in the woods.
As if something were there, besides the fermented cud
of a high-pitched scream under the hunter's moon.
Yes, I can balance a checkbook like a junior accountant.
And every time I get the garbage out on time, the neighbors
applaud my comeback, the curtains fluttering open
to welcome me back, righteous and industrious, into the fold.

And you, my son, think you're the conductor of the world,
make me stop at all the crossings. You tighten your fists
and tremble, to see something straight, and strong,
and full of steel, going on and on like that.
I don't have the heart to tell you, that it's all a dream.
That these trains weigh so damn much, you can put down
a wish, or handful of pennies, on the shiny tracks,

and the engines will hurtle by and crush them all.
But if you're lucky son, should you win the lotto,
or the Irish Sweepstakes, you might find one some day.
It'll be flattened out in the oily grass, or slipped down
between the splintered ties, Lincoln's war-pocked face
smooth as a baby's ass. Let me tell you, it ain't good for much.
You can carry it around I guess, drill a hole in it and wear
it on a string around your neck. Show it to the nurse
when she comes in to bathe you. You can hold it up to the light
and say, "Look at this, honey, look what happened a long time ago."
Then maybe so impressed, she'll stop and let the sponge linger,
as if to say, "Old man, your life's been such a miracle!"
The cool drops falling down between your thighs.

"FORTY MILLION NEW GALAXIES DISCOVERED"

1.

Finally. Those blank spots, all that lost matter
that I'd lie in bed and wonder about, explained.
So I go out to the plum tree on this inherited plot,
where Skip, my black border collie, is buried.
I want to tell him, for I am afraid he worried too,
trying to heal me with his hot moist salts,
when the universe was my bed, and the lights went out,
and he was the only thing I could reach for.
But I know the plum tree is gone. One would have to know
where it grew to see the rotted stump of what remains.
To have known this yard, to have had a father who polished
each blue-green blade of grass, and to know the house,
the center of which, he nailed himself further and further into.
To know the hermit crab he blew on, to see it wave
its claws and peek out at the bricks and the jonquils,
and the wren boxes overflowing with twigs and paper.
One by one, wife, success, dignity, my father lost all that mattered,
a prisoner of each trill and chirping bug-eyed squirrel
that chased its tail around the hundred-year-old maple.
And, yes, I am overjoyed at this discovery in space,
the ground lenses turning, grinding in focus, reaffirming
as only science can, that we are hardly as important
as this stump, this rotted spindly tree, I can still imagine
with its sour, silver plums that for twenty years no one ate.

2.

My sweet unbelieving daughter, dreaming in her cradle of vowels,
she smells like berries, but this is not enough they say.
They insist on lifting her this Sunday, mumbling and signing
the shadow of a cross on the center of her forehead.
To save her from the original cracked smell of her lover
yet to come, his juice disappearing from under her fingernails.
I desire your head on my shoulder, sweet girl, think how far removed
you are from God, all your brothers and sisters he has to watch over,
their red nubs and flowers gushing out of all these new galaxies.
"We are truly blessed," they say. But the only time I see God,
it's the back of his head, just when he is leaving some grave.
I must look just like him, though, because eventually they always
say, Thank God, when I am going. It must be the back of my head
    that reminds
them of faith, the thing we look for below the cherry burns of
    cigarettes
on a baby's skin, or the Guatemalan maid at the bus stop,
fingering the pocketful of her son's beaten-out teeth. But no matter.
For all that was missing is there now. In some vale of plum trees,
by a white stone cottage on some green postage stamp of a country,
in one of these forty million galaxies, there stands God's well.
And each of us in turn will have the chance to hand-crank the
    bucket
of Him, up and up and up, then bring it to our parched lips
    and be forgiven.

≡ THE AUTHOR ≡

William Loran Smith is the author of two chap-
books of poetry, *The Boy Who Became a Book* and
Avernus. His work has been recorded on *Omphalos,*
a spoken word CD. Smith has received numerous
scholarships and grants from the University of
Louisville and the University of Michigan. He is
currently finishing his MFA at Vermont College.
He lives with his wife and three children in
Louisville, Kentucky.